Sports Poems

Selected by John Foster

First published in the United States of America in 2008 by
dingles & company
P.O. Box 508
Sea Girt, New Jersey 08750

First Printing

Website: www.dingles.com

E-mail: info@dingles.com

Library of Congress Catalog Card No.: 2007907156

ISBN: 978-1-59646-618-0 (library binding)
　　　　978-1-59646-619-7 (paperback)

© Oxford University Press
This U.S. edition of *Sports Poems*, originally published in English in 1991, is published by arrangement with Oxford University Press.

Acknowledgments
The editor and publisher wish to thank the following who have kindly given permission for the use of copyright material:

Finola Akister for "Egg and Spoon Race", © Finola Akister 1990
Mary Dawson for "Obstacle Race", © Mary Dawson 1990
Michael Glover for "Racing the Wind", © Michael Glover 1990
Theresa Heine for "Sports Day", © Theresa Heine 1990
Brian Moses for "The Wheelchair Race", © Brian Moses 1990
Judith Nicholls for "Sack Race", © Judith Nicholls 1990
Johnson and Alcock Ltd. for Max Fatchen: "Just When..." from *Wry Rhymes for Troublesome Times* (Kestrel Books, 1983), © Max Fatchen 1983
Irene Yates for "The Flying Reptiles Race" and "The Fastest Runner", both © Irene Yates 1990

Illustrations by
Anthony Rule; Bucket; Norman Johnson; Peet Ellison;
David Parkins; Alex Brychta; Joe Wright

Printed in China

dingles & company

Obstacle Race

Over the tree trunks, under the net,
crossing the stream without getting wet;
over the planks on their hands and knees,
and wriggling through tires that hang from trees.
Then running uphill to the end of the track;
and a prize for the team that's first to get back.

Mary Dawson

Sack Race

Toes in,
knees in.
Quick now,
squeeze in!
Itchy back,
tickle knees,
hairy sack
makes you sneeze.
Two-feet-hop,
never stop!
Snap, snip,
don't trip . . .
There and back
jumping sack . . .
One . . .
   two . . .
      three . . .

        OFF!

Judith Nicholls

Racing the Wind

I said to the wind –
"I'll race you then
to that gate there
and back again!"
But the wind said to me –
"How will we tell
which of us won?
I'm invisible!"
So I thought and thought,
and then I found
a potato-chip bag
crumpled on the ground.
I picked it up
and said to the wind –
"You blow *this*
and I'll just run . . ."

So off we went,
me and that bag,
dashing like mad,
not once looking back.
But when we got there
the bag went on,
bouncing, flying
right across
the playing fields
till it got lost.
Well, I raced back
to the starting line,
shouting, "I've won!
Your bag can't run
in a straight line!"
The wind just didn't know
what to say.
It huffed and puffed
and gruffed around,
rattling the chimneypipes
all day,
blowing across and around and down,
searching for the bag it lost . . .

Michael Glover

The Flying Reptiles Race

Five flying reptiles were just about to dine.
The dinner had arrived, and it looked just fine.
Then up jumped a bossy one and shouted with glee,
"I bet that I could beat you to the Faraway Tree!"

The other reptiles laughed and they cried, "No way!
We're the fastest in the land, we could beat you any day!"
The bossy one boasted, "I am the fastest one!"
But they all disagreed. So the race was on.

They lined up on the cliff edge ready to begin.
Five flying reptiles, each saying, "I'll win!"
They gazed across the ocean stretching far beyond the sand.
"The winner," said the bossy one, "is first back to land."

8

Then "Go!" screeched the bossy one, giving them a fright –
and four foolish reptiles flew off into the night.
One bossy, greedy reptile went off alone to dine.
"They won't be back till dawn," he said. "The dinner is all mine!"

Irene Yates

The Wheelchair Race

We were side by side in the corridor,
trying to pass the time,
talking about what we both enjoyed,
his chair parked next to mine.

He showed me how well he whistled.
I told him my drawing was ace.
He asked how fast I could move.
I forgot who suggested a race!

He counted us down to zero.
"No dirty tricks," I said.
We sped along the polished floor.
I made the turn ahead.

We narrowly missed two cleaning ladies,
a nurse and an angry crew,
then knocked a tea cart sideways,
"Look out, it's the terrible two!"

Our doctor stepped out of his room
to check the dreadful din.
"You might have hurt yourselves," he said,
but smiled as we wheeled ourselves in.

Brian Moses

11

Sports Day

My teacher said, "Everyone,
just do your best.
Run as fast as you can,
and try to beat the rest."

And I ran really fast
till my legs nearly dropped,
and I reached the white tape
where they told us to stop.

And my teacher was there,
and she smiled and she said,
"You did run well, Peter,"
and she patted my head.

And she reached in a bag
and she gave a rosette
to Thomas MacGregor,
to Paul and to Brett.

And I stood there and waited
for her to reach in—
into the bag, and give me
a rosette with a pin.

But she just said, "Please, Peter,
go back to your place.
I have to watch out now
who wins the next race."

And I went slowly back.
I had not won a thing
to take home to my dad,
no rosette with a pin.

But worse than not pinning
a rosette to my chest
was to see Wayne O'Rourke
wearing *two* on his vest!

Theresa Heine

13

Egg and Spoon Race

When I entered the egg and spoon race,
I knew I was not very quick.
I couldn't run fast so I came in last
and my egg had hatched into a chick.

Finola Akister

The Fastest Runner

Sports day at school
was ever such fun –
the moms had a race
and who d'you think won?

MY MOM!

Irene Yates

Just When . . .

It's always the same.
Just when you're playing a game,
just when it's exciting
and interesting
with everyone racing
and chasing,
just when you're having so much fun,
somebody always wants something done!

Max Fatchen

Mouse Poems

Selected by John Foster

First published in the United States of America in 2008 by
dingles & company
P.O. Box 508
Sea Girt, New Jersey 08750

First Printing

Website: www.dingles.com

E-mail: info@dingles.com

Library of Congress Catalog Card No.: 2007907156

ISBN: 978-1-59646-618-0 (library binding)
       978-1-59646-619-7 (paperback)

© Oxford University Press
This U.S. edition of *Mouse Poems*, originally published in English in 1991, is published by arrangement with Oxford University Press.

Acknowledgments
The editor and publisher wish to thank the following who have kindly given permission for the use of copyright material:

Mary Dawson for "Ginger Cat", © Mary Dawson 1990
Eric Finney for "Mouse and Lion", © Eric Finney 1990
John Foster for "In The Middle of the Night", © John Foster 1990
Jean Kenward for "The House's Tale", © Jean Kenward 1990
Irene Rawnsley for "The Brave Mouse" and "Two Mice",
both © Irene Rawnsley 1990
John Rice for "A Mouse in the Kitchen", © John Rice 1990

Illustrations by
Eric Smith; Jenny Williams; Frances Cony; Bob Dewar;
Rowan Barnes-Murphy; Martin Ursell; Rowan Clifford

Printed in China

In the Middle of the Night

In the middle of the night,
while we slept,
the mouse crept
out of the nest
beneath the floor boards.

In the middle of the night,
while everything was quiet,
the mouse scampered
across the kitchen floor,
searching for bread crumbs.

In the middle of the night,
while Mom and Dad slept,
I crept
quietly down the stairs
to get myself a drink.

In the middle of the night,
when I opened the door
of the kitchen,
I saw a flash of fur
as a small brown mouse
shot past me.

And I jumped with fright
in the middle of the night.

John Foster

19

Jenny Williams 198

The House's Tale

This is the HOUSE
that was built in the road
where SAM lives.

These are the BRICKS
that made the house
that was built in the road
where SAM lives.

This is the STRAW
that packed the bricks
that made the house
that was built in the road
where SAM lives.

This is the TRUCK
that carried the bricks
(all packed in straw)
that made the house
that was built in the road
where SAM lives.

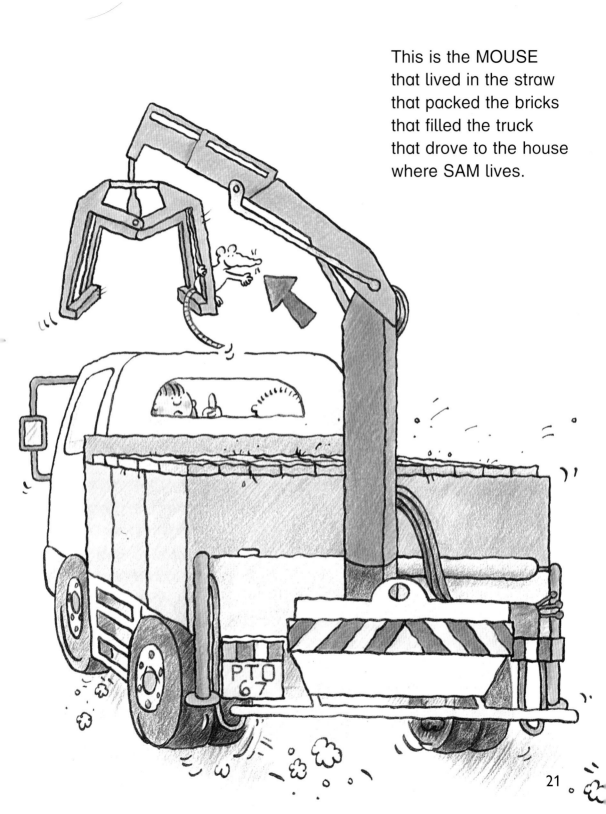

This is the MOUSE
that lived in the straw
that packed the bricks
that filled the truck
that drove to the house
where SAM lives.

21

He jumped and jittered
from paw to paw,
he hurried and scurried...
He peeped and saw
a roof, a window,
an open door
and tables and chairs,
and on the floor
some cookie crumbs
and an apple core
in the house in the road
where SAM lives.

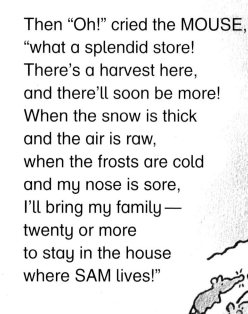

Then "Oh!" cried the MOUSE,
"what a splendid store!
There's a harvest here,
and there'll soon be more!
When the snow is thick
and the air is raw,
when the frosts are cold
and my nose is sore,
I'll bring my family—
twenty or more
to stay in the house
where SAM lives!"

So the MICE arrived
one winter's night
when the moon was full
and the stars were bright
and the Christmas angels
took their flight.
They all crept in
from left and right
to stay in the house
where SAM lives.
Did ever you see
such a splendid sight?
Just LOOK at the HOUSE —
the family house —
that was built in the road
where SAM lives!

Jean Kenward

23

Ginger Cat

Sandy and whiskered, the ginger cat
sniffs around the corners for a mouse or a rat;
creeping right under the cupboard he sees
a little mouse having a nibble of cheese.

On velvety paws with hardly a sound
the ginger cat watches, and padding around
he finds a good hiding place under a chair
and sits like a statue not moving a hair.

Then baring his claws from their velvety sheath,
he pounces, meowing through threatening teeth.
But the cat is too late, for the sensible mouse
was eating the cheese at the door of his house.

Mary Dawson

A Mouse in the Kitchen

There's a mouse in the kitchen
  playing skittles with the peas.
He's drinking mugs of coffee
  and eating last week's cheese.

There's a mouse in the kitchen;
  we could catch him in a hat,
otherwise he'll toast the biscuits
  and that's bound to annoy the cat.

There's a mouse in the kitchen
  ignoring all our wishes,
He's eaten tomorrow's dinner,
  but at least he's washed the dishes.

John Rice

Mouse and Lion

A mouse caught by a lion
pleads for his life,
begs to go home
to his children and wife:
"You never know, Leo,
if you set me free
one day you might get
in a fix and need me."
Leo, amused by
the field mouse's lip,
lets him go. He departs
with a squeak and a skip.
And, would you believe it,
the very next week
Leo the lion
just happens to get
hopelessly tangled in
a game hunters' net.
Mouse happens along,
says, "I'm small, with no roar,
but there's one thing I can do,
and that is to gnaw."
In less than an hour
the net's nibbled through...

Do someone a good turn,
he might do one for you.

Eric Finney

Two Mice

Two mice lived
in a garden wall;
she made a warm nest,
he found a hole.

One wore a gray coat,
the other a brown;
she liked country,
he liked town.

He ate bacon,
she ate barley;
he slept late,
but she woke early.

Every night when
people were in bed,
he searched for a supper
of bacon and bread.

She ate each morning
when the dew was wet;
and so, these
two mice never met.

Irene Rawnsley

The Brave Mouse

Annabel,
Annabel,
come and see here;
a mouse is asleep
in tabby cat's ear!

He climbed up her tail
as she lay in a heap;
ran over her body,
then fell fast asleep.

I wonder,
I wonder,
for brown mouse's sake,
if he or if tabby
will be first awake?

Irene Rawnsley